THE
NEW KINGDOM

The
New Kingdom
A New Play of Ancient Times

EMMANUEL PAUL

iUniverse, Inc.
Bloomington

The New Kingdom
A New Play of Ancient Times

iUniverse books may be ordered through booksellers or by contacting:

iUniverse
1663 Liberty Drive
Bloomington, IN 47403
www.iuniverse.com
1-800-Authors (1-800-288-4677)

ISBN: 978-1-4620-2708-8 (sc)
ISBN: 978-1-4620-2710-1 (hc)
ISBN: 978-1-4620-2709-5 (ebk)

Library of Congress Control Number: 2011913277

Printed in the United States of America

iUniverse rev. date: 08/04/2011

Synopsis

It is 1540 BC; Egypt has been divided since the invasion
of the Hyksos—a band of nomadic warriors roaming from
land to land with a base in Palestine. They occupy the north,
known as lower Egypt and have spent a hundred or so years
of war and truce with the once mighty Pharaohs who have
now been pushed from their former capital in Avaris to a
new seat of power in Thebes in the south, known as upper
Egypt.

The Thebans have lost great Pharaohs in the struggles
including the brother and the father of Ahmose. Ahmose
rises from being a young prince sharing power with his
powerful mother Aahotep, to be one of the greatest Pharaohs
ever; freeing his people from the invaders, uniting Egypt
under one rule, quelling a religious uprising and bringing
the divided land of Nubia under a new kingdom and rule
to ensure its continued peace and prosperity. This period of
struggle and reunification represents the 18th Dynasty of the
Pharaohs known also as *The New Kingdom.*

Glossary

Hut-waret: Avaris

Waset: Thebes

Kemet: Egypt, Egyptian

Lower Egypt: northern Egypt

Upper Egypt: southern Egypt

Peoples of the north: Egyptians living in the north of Egypt

Abju: Abydos

Ta-Sety: Land of the bow (formerly Nubia present day Sudan)

Kush: area covering lower (northern) Nubia

Kushite: Nubian (present day Sudanese)

Kerma: a region of lower (northern) Nubia

Narmer: Pharaoh considered to be the unifier of Egypt and
    founder of 1st Dynasty

Asiatics, Semites: Used by the ancient Egyptians to refer to
    the middle east and the people residing in that region

Nebpehtyre: The Lord of Strength is Re

All-knowing One: the Egyptian Oracle—a Seer who provides
    predictions of the future

Perfuming of the mouth: lunch

Aser: Osiris

Heru: Horus

Ibu: Place of purification, where mummification is performed

Opet: Festival to celebrate the anniversary when the King's right to rule was re-confirmed

Cast of Characters

Theban royal family
King Ahmose I
Queen Aahotep: mother to Ahmose I
Ahmose-Nefertare: sister to King Ahmose I
Tetisheri: grandmother to King Ahmose I
Ahmes-Merytamun: former queen to King Kamose

Hyksos King
King Apopi II

Kerma King
King Nedjeh: King of Kerma

Others
Priest Ani: a Theban priest
Priest Tetian: a Kushite Priest & cousin to Priest Ani
Commander Turi: Head Commander of King Ahmose' armies
Miofylo: a boy citizen
Other Officials, Embalmer, Servants, Scribe, Councillors, Priestesses, Seer

Prologue

Λ Temple in Waset

[Enter Priest Ani]

Priest Ani:

>This century past, how bleeds this noble land,
>Under the burden of these foreign clans!
>Rebellious maids and war-mongering serfs,
>Stand ever ready with blood lust to usurp.
>A stranger sleeps where virtue had its place,
>And stains with blood our ancient laws of Grace.
>We call upon thee Re bring forth our saviour;
>Or be damned Kemet in this our gravest hour!
>T'is Seth's reign: the rich become the poor,
>Men quick to anger and quicker still to war.
>Young, feebled women pregnant with hollow seeds,
>Face food-starved children wilting like weeds.
>Gone are all the laughter and all song,
>Replaced with death and evil wrong,
>A cheerful pest embraces the earth's crust,
>Reducing cattle to nothing more than dust.

And eating swine has driven men to rage,
Whilst rivers, hued red, are spewing plague;
Poisoning trees and bush with barrenness;
So driving the God-Bird from his age-old nest.
The King respects no word, nor word the King;
A puppet symbol only, reflecting.
As brother now stays not to slay his brother,
Rape, pillage and dishonour his mother,
Steal greedily what belongs to King,
To beg favors and rejoice in sin.
The southern masses which once before us kneed;
Now seek alliances with another breed.
Suspicion reigns where once there was sweet love.
How to throw off this cloak of foreign stuff?
We, people of Kemet, a proud and noble race;
Are now brought low and made ignoble-base.

[Exit]

Act 1 Scene 1

Λ palace in Waset

[The scene is set in the glamorous royal chamber of Tetisheri, mother to Queen Aahotep and grandmother to Ahmose. Present are: Tetisheri, Queen Aahotep, Princess Nefertere, Ahmes-Merytamun, Ahmose and female servants. Ahmose sits at the bedside of Tetisheri]

Tetisheri:

[Who is lying in bed speaks to Ahmose]

Young Lord, lay your hand on this place, what rhythm do you feel?

Ahmose:

I feel the beating of your heart Queen's Mother.

Tetisheri:

> And should you lay your head here, you would hear a heart beat. Soon, this rhythm will stop and I shall depart this world to enter another. This world I enter is the Afterworld: the Kingdom of the gods—Re's mighty realm. In this after world, the gods do watch us and judge us and only the worthy pass. Re is the king of the gods and you must know that you are his son.

Ahmose:

> But am I not of Sequenre's blood?

Tetisheri:

> Indeed, Sequenre was your earthly father but once you became King, Re claimed you as his and you follow only his teachings. He also speaks to you and us through the All-knowing One; which guides us and keeps our enemies from our door. Little one, I fear not my passing and we as a people fear not death; it is a natural journey that all must take and we all aspire to be godly, with everlasting strength, everlasting peace. When I pass let joyous song follow me on my path, not woeful tears.

Ahmose:

> Can I follow you but yet return?

Tetisheri:

> No, there is no passing back from that to this. The
> Kingdom of Re is the final place. First though,
> you must serve your peoples for they need you and
> though I shall not see the day when you become a
> man yet I do know you will be just. This divided
> land we know as Kemet must again be whole and
> the people one. Our people worship false icons
> whilst bandits feed off the bounties of the Nile.
> What good to be this black and bold when we
> have no soul. In this life I have known nothing
> but the struggle to preserve our sense of grace. I
> have fought and I have killed many enemies. I
> saw my Lords fall; I was insulted and became a
> nothing. Our people vanished and our enemies
> laughed to see the lion tamed and naked. The
> bitterness I have is not with the deaths of my kin
> but their unfulfillment and disgrace. I feel such
> sadness for our peoples; forced from their homes
> and made to honour those less worthy. We pay not
> just in monies but in blood. What price honour,
> what price spirit, what price history! You Ahmose,
> young King, young warrior, are the defender of
> our ways. Should the world know Kemet was built
> by Asiatics? For will they not claim our glories as
> their own? And how might this then be disproved
> when time will create a vagueness cloaking reality.

3

Ahmose:

> Will our writings not speak of the truth?

Tetisheri:

> They will destroy all or re-form our words. Already they have begun to write our history with their gods. Soon their history will be our history; soon our wealth will be their wealth. Should they continue, our ways shall be lost forever and their ways shall prevail. Who commands the capital commands the glory. We are a great people risen from the great tribes of the south our legacy follows the great river and will one day be buried with it. But until that day they must know us, they must see us.

Ahmose:

> I shall make them remember, Queen's Mother. I shall make them see us.

> [Exit]

Act 1 Scene 2

Thɾonε ɾoom aτ huτ-waɾeτ

[Enter Apopi and Councillor]

Apopi:

How is the world Councillor?

Councillor:

Mighty One, our ears in Waset speak of much unrest and I do fear the blacks may rise again under the boy King Ahmose.

Apopi:

And should I fear! Should they rise again then shall we smite them yet again; as my father did the rude Sequenre and his whelp Kamose. The peoples of the north are comfortable with our ways and enjoy a peace and prosperity, however they might try to rouse the crowds with tales of chaos and destruction come again.

Councillor:

> They will ever seek to steal command and amongst
> their boastful tribe they whisper words of "unity"
> and "Narmer" and we are seen as nothing more
> than "foreigners" and "usurpers". Yes, we have the
> capital and command but support from all the
> peoples of this land is divided. It does not suffice
> our advanced techniques; for those advantages
> that we once did hold are no longer ours to
> command alone. We must be mindful and trust
> not to complacency.

Apopi:

> Then we can seek our brothers in the Palestine,
> as before. The boy Ahmose is too weak to lead,
> which gives us time to see which way they bend.

Councillor:

> I fear that queen. She incites the folk to stir and
> does make them uneasy in their state. It was not
> wise to allow this truce.

Apopi:

> So, the queen, she that rules until he comes of age
> has but an embittered heart and seeks to avenge a
> husband and a son's death on the field. She may

bleat but never yet was a woman's rant the fear of kings.

Councillor:

Let us consider rebuilding old alliances, for what we cannot achieve with greater weaponry must we achieve with greater numbers. We must re-forge those unions with the enemies of Ahmose. The white mercenaries care not who they fight and the Kush straining under the Kemet whip seek to unify all the peoples of Ta-Sety.

Apopi:

So . . . so, but the Kush has long now been under the Kemet thumb and they have none to stand against the King. Also, can they be trusted to stand against old allies? For I do remember the Medjay at Kamose's side.

Councillor:

There is a chief, of commanding stature, who leads a tribe never subjected by the Kemet. He speaks the honeyed words of unity and wealth. His tribe's skill in warfare is well known, which in this period of uncertainty and weakness may break the King. This presents for us an opportunity; a pact with them on terms agreed would help secure true unity of this land. It is better now to act and seek support, for this might spur them on to start some action. He holds in Kerma and his peoples call him Nedjeh.

Apopi:

Well, then let us send correspondence to this chief and arrange some talks I think to make a deal.

[Exit Councillor]

The Councillor's words are true: there has of late been restlessness in Waset, which I ignored not seeing much in these activities. I have the capital and command and they but words. I see though we must quickly act to curb some rebel spirits. I know this land is tamed but it is not one, which in itself breeds discontentment. Yet all peoples must look forward now and in that future they shall know it is Apopi who rules Kemet. We are not foreign to this realm; ever have we known this place and ever shall we own it. Ever shall history favour the strong and ever the weak shall bear the brunt of sacrifice. Should I deny my natural inclinations to own, to build, to live and breathe where I have lived and breathed. Their world is dying and we should not allow the decay to be prolonged but finish this matter quickly. Had I been bolder, we should now rule from north to south. Instead, I allowed them space to fester in the upper lands. I know I have not judged this matter wrong, yet I did not reckon with Aahotep but should have from the tales of Tetisheri; as coming from that line of warrior queens. But by all the Gods I swear this queen shall know her place before my end is done!

[Exit]

Act 1 Scene 3

A Temple in Waset

[Enter Priestess and Miofylo]

Priestess:

Take you the statue of Amun and apply the
ointment so, next that of Mut and lastly Khonsu.
A good application should last you half an hour.

Miofylo:

Yes, Priestess.

Priestess:

See first to the disrobing of the statues and then to
the application of the oils.

Miofylo:

Yes, Priestess.

Priestess:

I do know your father, boy?

Miofylo:

> My father works with stone, Priestess. It is likely these statues are his work

Priestess:

> So you are Chuba's son. And you would follow him after your time with us or would you rather join the Priesthood?

Miofylo:

> I do prefer the study of the Gods. Though my father thinks me idle and a dreamer and seeks for me a "manly" occupation. But I am not content with what he wants for me.

Priestess:

> You must heed well the advice of your parents for they do know you best. So now, look to your tasks.

Miofylo:

> Though I feel different? He would have me work my hands but not my head.

Priestess:

> Hands too have their purpose.

Miofylo:

> I thirst for knowledge, there is so much I need to know, so many questions for which I seek the answers. I wonder at the Gods, our being, the purpose to our lives. I cannot find these answers forming stone.

Priestess:

> Ah . . . the thirst for knowledge so raw and wild in the young. Youth, you do not know your place? Yet, should you know it, would you accept it or question further. Youngling, the thirst for knowledge is never satisfied; nor should this be, nor can this be. Everything must be questioned and we the teachers must answer you. So knowledge is not lost but returned changed, reformed, added to and re-taught. Why should we learn to form words if knowledge should be lost.

Miofylo:

> Can I learn now whilst I do my chores?

Priestess:

> What knowledge should I now divulge to quench your thirst?

Miofylo:

> How came we here? Why are we here?

Priestess:

> How came we here, what is our purpose here; In the beginning there were no gods there was no Kemet, there was nothing but chaos. There was no thing but the mighty elements who unable to bring order amongst themselves allowed nothing to be. From this disorder finally came one powerful element god into being; the mightiest element god of them all for through him came our world into being and he breathed life on earth and brought order and allowed things to exist and take form. We know and see him as the sun and watch him rise and fall each day as he crosses the sky in the boat of a million years. We speak his name, Re, and worship his many forms of transformation. Those transformations touch us and mould us. Through Re came the first earthly gods into being: Aser and Isis and from them came Heru the guardian of our world. Their history of loss, struggle and triumph is also our history. A story repeated a million times in a million lives with a million variations; Aser killed by his brother Seth became the ruler of the kingdom of the dead. Heru, our earthly guardian, was saved from the evil Seth for Isis hid him

amongst the Buto marshes where he was found and cared for by a wet-nurse and was able to defeat his uncle in Re's court and reclaim the kingdom of the living. So was our world saved and so on life went. Soon came we into being for Re in his wisdom recognised a role for people in this great story.

Miofylo:

Then we too are godly?

Priestess:

We did lose our godliness and became ordinary; as a lesson for us to earn this state through honest living. You should know your purpose then is to regain this in the kingdom of Re. For though death does claim us all not all shall gain access to his kingdom unchallenged.

Miofylo:

How can we enter Re's kingdom?

Priestess:

In Re's greatness he did leave us with the means to again become godly and join him in his realm: this path is through His Majesties. His Majesties must continue to worship Re and follow the teachings of Re, defeat the enemies of Re and ensure their peoples understand Re's preachings. This means Pharaoh. Should the mighty Pharaohs fail in this or be ignored by the gods or in any way displease the gods, then we are damned and cannot gain godly ascendancy. Darkness will descend on us and we would depart this world and without body or soul enter the underworld; where tortuous demons await to devour our eternal soul.

Miofylo:

Should I be re-born after death? How might I be worthy?

Priestess:

See you that parchment Khonsu holds before him these are Maat's laws, read on!

Miofylo:

[Reading]

That you might not do falsehood against men;
That you might do no evil;
That you might not take life;
That you might not command to kill;
That you might not oppose a god in his procession;

That you might do no wrong in the place of truth;
That you might not do what the gods detest;
That you might not make suffering for anyone;
That you might not misbehave;
That you might not be cruel to man or beast

Priestess:

This young one is your path to re-birth. For at your passing you shall be judged and should your heart be true Aser will return you to his kingdom. But should you prove false the great devourer shall take your soul and you shall spend torturous eternity amongst others equally unworthy. We are all ordinary servants of the gods who bend to their whims; when they send us floods we cannot work, when they send us plagues we cannot eat, when they send us enemies we cannot grow. Yet they send us kings to lead us back. Here we do much that is customary and ordinary; much cleaning and preparation, for ceremonies dedicated to the gods. We cannot neglect our tasks for that in turn would be to neglect the gods and their anger would be a thing terrible to behold. It is His Majesty who does spread the godly word or so commands, for it is he who embodies all divinity. But your time with us will make these matters clear. I must leave you now but do not tarry with your work.

Miofylo:

But there are so many gods.

Priestess:

We beings need guidance, we need their presence to help us daily. Can fewer gods truly take care of so many of us and all our earthly demands. We follow the actions commanded by all the gods: Maat's laws give us order, Thoth gives us knowledge, Anup guides our death. But now to work, for more you'll know tomorrow in the class.

[Exit]

Act 1 Scene 4

Throne room at Waset

[Ahmose and Aahotep are sitting on the throne, an Embalmer and messenger are present, also servants]

Aahotep:

> To you Priest, we seek the news of the embalming of Great Queen's mother. Disturbing reports of death and distress have reached our ears. What did transpire in The Good House, speak!

Embalmer:

> Oh great Queen, it did not begin well. Our ibu was well secured near the tomb and a huge throng had gathered due to the announcement. There was much wailing as is custom still all was calm. Not long after the cutter made his mark as instructed by the Scribe was he then lost to us.

Aahotep:

> Lost . . . how lost?

Embalmer:

> Soon after he had done his work, stones rained down on him and the people screamed "sinner" and "defiler of souls" that he should harm another who had done him no wrong.

Aahotep:

> Had we not instructed guards in the protection of the ceremony? Stoned to death you say?

Embalmer:

> It was not the stones themselves for they were few, the man being of a sensitive age had a great fright. I fear his heart gave out.

Aahotep:

> Well . . . well . . . poor soul. And then?

Embalmer:

> I consigned all the organs to the four guardians in readiness for the journey. Imset will ensure the liver's health, Ha'py that of the lungs. Duamutef the stomach and Qebehsenuf the intestines. All are now protected. With the removal of the brain I

feared again. I heard one woman cry, "the demon's hook!", as I readied to remove the useless organ from the head. They stirred again. The people's ignorance is unsettling. Perhaps we priests should seek to impart a better understanding of this preparation.

Aahotep:

Those that are ignorant will always remain so. Was all then well?

Embalmer:

The water was scarce, I was unable to wash the body as best I could. As I sought to leave to fetch some new supplies my way was barred by some who spat and insulted me. What evil practices was occurring here with those no longer living, what abuses and what dishonour, were their questions. Should a priest's honor be of question?

Aahotep:

Some have been foul. Was the water fetched and the ceremony completed?

Embalmer:

The ceremony was completed as is the tradition handed down to me and testimony of some hundred mummified. Great Queen Mother was prepared with oil and scents and lastly filled with dried materials. Now being laid to dry some 40 days. In three score days and 10 is the embalming then complete with further washings, the divine wrapping and magic spells spoken. Once all embalmment is complete, so can the final ceremony be performed.

Aahotep:

I have heard this process done in much a shorter time. Not that you seek more finances for less craft

Embalmer:

The danger, oh Great Queen, is then to provide a workmanship of a lesser quality. Only, after years is this often revealed.

Ahmose:

Why is the body filled, why the oils and scents?

Embalmer:

Not that it be too stiff and unwelcoming but have the texture and beauty as it had when it was full of earthly life and necessary to again be lived in in the After-life

Aahotep:

> Therefore, all is done just before the Opet fest.
> Thus merriment can follow this mournful time.
> We shall attend in seventy days the final ceremony
> of the Opening of the Mouth. Look that all is
> done in time. You may leave us

[Exit Embalmer]

> And now to you Messenger, what news have you?

Messenger:

> Great Queen, this bound for the clans in Kerma
> was intercepted by our forces

Aahotep:

> Read on!

Messenger:

[Reading]

> *Greetings Chieftain of Kush oh great Nedjeh! I
> Awoserre, the son of Re, Apopi chieftain of Hut-waret
> wonder why you have arisen as chieftain without
> letting me know. Have you not beheld what the
> Kemet has done against us devastating our two lands?*

> *The boy king Ahmose respects not you or I. Come!*
> *Fare north at once, do not be timid. Let us sit and*
> *discuss like brothers. He shall not trouble you, I shall*
> *hold him aside. Come quick!*

> *Apopi`*

Aahotep:

Give me the message here, you may leave us

[Exit Messenger]

Ahmose:

What should this mean Great Mother?

Aahotep:

My curses rain on them! The Hyksos seek alliances against us. They mean to strike to steal yet more of that which does not belong to them. We must strike first we can no longer hold! How meaningless are these words of peace! We shall send their craven hides back to that hole from which they crawled! Let us use this treachery well to rouse the crowds, for many of whom the memory of Kamose's fall still fuels anger. We shall avenge him, my fallen Lord, the theft of our heritage and unite this land once more to honor the first amongst us to unite the two crowns. Oh Narmer, let not your victory have been in vain! Help us evict these thieves. Have they not suppressed us into this nothingness state in which we live, subjecting our peoples to humiliation and false Gods, creating this nest of Asiatics in our midst. What good to be this black and bold when this pestilence spoils your bread, steals your dignity, claims your greatness and pales your history.

Ahmose:

I think we can count on many from the north still not accepting Hyksos rule joining our campaign when it begins. We must simply reawaken their conscience.

Aahotep:

This is so. We need a confirmation of this campaign to spirit our peoples. Our priests shall see that the All-Knowing One delivers a message of hope and victory to our folk.

[Exit all]

Act 1 Scene 5

At Hut-waret a field of battle, sounds of warfare.
The war with the Hyksos has been raging
for some 5 years

[Enter Ahmose, Aahotep and Turi in chariots]

Turi:

They weaken, through the length of the siege.

Aahotep:

Do you see Great One this day is ours! See how the bowmen's aim is true. So well have we mastered their new weaponry it now serves our cause better than theirs. We mastered but kept the best of us and now strike hard and true.

Ahmose:

They thought us defeated and weak so giving us the upper hand. [Cries] Their walls are breached!

Turi:

> Shaquar now leads the soldiers in, My Majesty.

Ahmose:

> Mother, the enemy retreats, may I ride?

Aahotep:

> Go, lead the chariots in attack, crush the invader but bring Apopi back.

> [Exit all except Aahotep. Sounds of horns]

Aahotep:

> Ah Ahmose, my son and lion that you are! You are the hope; that flame to light our way. All Kemet will bow at your feet if you bring glory back. Your bold but rash brother did attempt to drive these foreigners off; but he was too quick to action and too slow to heed. In you I see another type, Ahmose Nebpehtyre! The invader did once beat us back with all his fineries of war, but no more. The Kingdom of Kemet was but a retreating lion laid low to lick its wounds but not defeated; and out of the chaos of those years we are reborn; stronger and wiser still, as the true rulers of Kemet the sons and daughters of Aser and Isis one children under the almighty Gods. Only through the

reawakening of our true spirit could we have this day. Never did we accept defeat or succumb to the Hyksos promises of peace, as they would have it. Their appeared acceptance of our gods, but just a method to appease the mass, giving a semblance of consistency; which in itself was just another tool to bend our people's reason to compliance; so that we would not see the darkness fall until the light was gone.

[Cheering and jubilant cries]
I think the fight be won for they return.

[Re-enter Ahmose holding Apopi's crown, Turi and soldiers with captive Apopi]

Ahmose:

King's Mother your prize!

[Hands crown to Aahotep]

Aahotep:

[Takes a moment to savour the crown and its significance]

What say you usurper to your spent force, to the glory that is the people of Kemet. Was this battle not well won?

Apopi:

Indeed Queen, today we were well beaten. Our techniques no longer foreign as you deem our presence, today becomes the student then the master.

Aahotep:

Forget you not; that teacher he was taught must teach. We are much older than yourselves from us came you to learn. As I stand before you here as queen and mother, robbed by your line of husband and child, I hold victory in the one hand and retribution in the other and your life hangs but by a word. You wanted to usurp our kingdom but instead have ended up a slave. Was this well thought? Did you ever in your arrogance think that such a thing could pass?

Apopi:

As the victor surveys the conquered before him knowing full well there is no turning back; does he show remorse or doubt about his adventure when he believes that right is on his side. Do you

Queen, on this day; believe that you would ever lose your kingdom?

Aahotep:

True, we are weakened and confused by your invasion, so on this day our glory is not full; only our conscience is returned complete. But that such a thing could pass I see it not, for is it not the abilities of a people to learn from its mistakes?

Apopi:

If they be able. Still, often though man learns from his mistakes, his memory is short. As to my case; we came to settle here not to destroy. The land of Kemet is known far and wide and musicians sing of the richness that is the Nile. We sort not to destroy but to learn the source of all this greatness, to be part of it and to be with many of our landsmen in one place. We were attracted by her awe and by her grace. I hope your judgement considers this.

Ahmose:

Consider this usurper; a people made fearful and ignorant of their past; take that from them and you steal their future. Were we not suffering under your foreign presence, were the royals not made puppets for the sake of wealth? Did you once consider the spirits of our peoples; did you once seek to heal this injured land?

Apopi:

We did not destroy young king and what you did learn from us, will stand you in good stead when future hoards would descend to take from you. It is assured that this will happen as surely as the scarab wakes the dead to rise. So in this contribution you should see a benefit.

Aahotep:

Destruction of the body or the mind is but the same. Also, the butcheries and the stress of war are not for us, we are a people promoting rather peace; we seek to glorify our gods but not ourselves, thankful for the blessing that is the Nile. Through us, our people know their past and know their future; this knowledge halts a restlessness of spirit. Take us from them and they become a nothing; losing that glorious path to Re's mighty kingdom. This is our pattern for life and After-life. But enough! Maat waits; for you Apopi shall not leave this field alive, so is the custom when a serf usurps. Also, the reckoning of my son, my husband and my husband's father fall on your line. As for your people, know you this; we shall rub them out or

spare them only if their will serve Re. This is the
verdict, it shall then be so!

[Exit all except Aahotep and Ahmose)

Aahotep:

My King, the words Apopi spoke have set me to
thinking that an answer is required on the issue of
security: must we forever fight to maintain it. Can
we ensure security through peace?

Ahmose:

I know not mother, but it seems to me that only
the strong can create the peace.

Aahotep:

Indeed, might these words be wise. Yet, let us look
for further answers from the All-Knowing One.

[Exit]

Act 1 Scene 6

A temple in Waset

[Enter Priest Ani and Priestesses]

Priest Ani:

> The King and Queen command this day a private audience with the All-Knowing One.

First Priestess:

> To what purpose, lord?

Priest Ani:

> To avoid a repetition of this terrible period; I hear Apopi's address fueled curiosity in the regal minds and they will a prediction that they hope is favorable to their cause; providing answers to the security of the realm.

Second Priestess:

> And our security, my lord?

Priest Ani:

> Indeed, my children, are we not pale shadows and religious relics conducting ceremonies but forbidden to preach. Our true roles are to enlighten spiritually but we are bound. Our gods demand our freedom and our peoples thirst.

Second Priestess:

> My lord, what should the All-Knowing One return?

Priest Ani:

> Let the Wise One resolve the uncertainty in the regal minds, which at this point may doubt some further action against the Palestine. It would be hoped that words of wisdom will confirm that war alone secures a peace. But should a peace be sought that is both lasting and fruitful then must the hand of Grace reach beyond the Nile to grab those fruits and strike those who should deny it. See to it, my children.

Both:

> We shall

> [Exit Priestesses]

Priest Ani:

    The priesthood's power must grow, this is certain. The King embodies the political and divine and all others are stripped of both. The crowning makes a man into a god, a god-man; the son of Re, but we the Priesthood remain religious symbols having mere duties but no authority. When the King dies; then breaks that godly link and the peoples are left powerless and godless—a weakened state. This absolute hold on absolute power is dangerous; our wealth and security but victim to the will and desire of the King; man or boy he is but human and subject to the errors that humans make. We will that we are answerable only to our gods and to none other. So, to avoid potential disaster to the Priesthood, so must it lead in priestly matters and the King must lead in matters pertaining to the state. The title of High Priest of Amun must be held by another; a priest of the highest rank as the true representative of the gods. The royals, in their inflated states, have not sensed our bitterness and suppression. Forever, tradition and history will be their claim but history is made by those who have the courage first to break tradition. Our gods fuel us, their work shall be done.

[Exit]

Act 1 Scene 7

[Present are Ahmose and Aahotep sitting on thrones, a Seer and guards]

Aahotep:

Come Seer let us hear the reading of the All-Knowing One.

Seer:

Having commanded the Wise One in the following:

What can ensure the kingdom that is Kemet

I have this:

[Reading]

From the Union of Shu and Tefnut
Came Glory's land,

And only the hand that passes can amend.
In journeys friend the stranger packs his gifts;
In journeys end are brought false promises:
The sacrifice of truth and mirror-like;
Replaced by icons of the Semite.
Therefore, as the hand accepts,
So must the head reject.
Seek not temptation of another's house;
Rejoice in this earth from which life comes.
Accept not the sweet words from a foreign throat;
Save only when it blesses Re the god.
All other peoples alien to yourselves,
Envy the bounties and treasures of this land.
Trust not a people who put women down;
Strength is the daughter who speaks Isis' name.
If these words are heard and seeds are sown,
Then Kemet will remain a Pharaoh's home.

So was it spoken

[Hands parchment to Queen Aahotep]

Aahotep:

We thank you, leave us.

[Exit Seer]

Ahmose:

> What say you mother, the All-Knowing One shows
> the way, were we to let the Hyksos grow again then
> envious of our wealth they would return forever to
> plague our people with *'false promises'*.

Aahotep:

> Yes, there is the danger from without. But we have
> many here in this land of Kemet who come from
> foreign parts. They are our subjects and they now
> work to make us strong and we have need of them.
> By accepting this, the danger lies within for soon
> they grow; as did some hostile folk who joined the
> Hyksos tribe, they were those who grew with us.
> Yet as I recall they may not be of us:
> [Quoting]
>
> *Accept not the sweet words from a foreign throat;*
> *Save only when it blesses Re the god*
>
> Had they been of us and spoke Re's name they
> never would have turned to blessing Baal. We
> always will have strangers in our midst but by
> knowing who rejects the word of Re we see the true
> face of our enemy. To give up our customs and our
> ways is the first step to decline and fall. So must
> we take measures in our hands to keep the foreign

41

populace in control not that the swelling foreign over-runs our folk. Then remains the enemy from without. They must know our strength to such a degree that they would ever fear return again.

Ahmose:

I shall drive the invader back and destroy his fortresses in the Palestine, no matter what the cost. This matter leave to me mother. On my return Kemet will have no fear and I shall lay the basis for real peace and wipe this shameful stain from our face.

Aahotep:

Ah, Ahmose! I once did see your face before your birth, in a dream. You held the double crown aloft, gleaming new. Yet you were sad. With your other hand you held a Kushite queen and spoke the words of healing and renewal.

Ahmose:

You never spoke to me of this before.

Aahotep:

The memory is with new hope refreshed. I wish it were no dream.

Ahmose:

But a Kushite queen, mother I think indeed
a dream. And why so sad when Kemet again is
one?

Aahotep:

The priestess thinks it means the opposite; as
our dream world is a mirror to the real, the mind
distorts as it reflects and one must read the symbols
in reverse.

Ahmose:

Well then mother, I'll take with me this hopeful
dream and convey its message to our soldiers
in the field and with it gender strength and
encouragement. And on my return you'll know it
was no dream.

Aahotep:

Fare you well, my son.

Ahmose:

And you good mother.

[Exit]

Act 1 Scene 8

A temple in Kerma

[Enter Priest Ani and Priest Tetian]

Priest Ani:

How goes your end, cousin?

Priest Tetian:

We gain from the ruins; Nedjeh commands the forces that seek to unleash a terrible destruction upon the Kemet. We the priesthood have consigned the godly blessing, for is it not evident a false kingship sits on the throne of Kemet; the gods send us plagues, war, loss and destruction. All these things have we endured and much more. No peoples have suffered as we; faceless and impotent, used yet deemed useless. The Pharaoh's throne is high and mighty his head tops the clouds blinding his feet.

Priest Ani:

It is true the Gods are unappeased and the Pharaoh unbending, so it falls to us to lead the sufferers into the light. It is true that we are bound in servitude when we should be teachers. These words are true and as they are true so is the Pharaoh false; false in deed and false in understanding. So are we right, so shall we convince, so shall we succeed.

Priest Tetian:

At this meeting all chiefs were agreed to the idea of independence. All agreed loyalty to Nedjeh. Yet all do fear the might of the Kemet.

Priest Ani:

Yes, but that might has relied in part on the Kush. United the peoples of Ta-Sety cannot fail. So with the fall of the Pharaohs begins the rise of the priesthood. Now is the time to strike now while Ahmose' forces are split to drive back the invader and the land still not healed.

Priest Tetian:

Rise cousin? How might we rise? As we have yet to set our will and mark our path. This course we follow though I believe it true, is full of danger and guarantees are none. This struggle we undertake to separate king and God is mighty and I fear the time is not yet ours.

Priest Ani:

Put away those fears; though we start what we might not finish yet is the conclusion assured. Our struggle is for the priesthood and it's survival and we must not deal in individual gains and victories. There must be one to throw the pebble in the lake to break the calm, we are that one.

Priest Tetian:

We have not convinced Nedjeh that true spiritual power rests with the priesthood. Do we not jump from one servitude to another?

Priest Ani:

The hold is weaker with the Kush, the belief paler. We can convince with time. The Pharaohs cannot change that much is certain. Yes, we seek new masters but in this new chapter we are no more the servant.

[Exit]

Act 2 Scene 1

A luxury room in the palace at Waset.
Ahmose's armies have been fighting
for some five years now in Palestine

[Nefertare and Ahmes are attended by servants.
Another is playing soft music on a harp]

Nefertare:

> Tell me more sister of the lot that is a women's towards her king.

Ahmes:

> For my part I see much fortune in this role. The king and queen symbol of unity; the brother and sister joined in matrimony from whence comes the line of great god-kings. So was it since the first great union so shall it always be. It is a role that honours women, we daughters of Isis are to bear the greatest gift—that of godly life.

Nefertare:

What demands had he of you that was our former king?

Ahmes:

To play the women and the queen, bring strength and virtue when dark moments come. I remember well those moments, sister, like a heavy cloud only now beginning to shift; as Apopi's hold on Kemet made us choke and tried to stifle words of encouragement and hope. Here is a woman at her strongest though and putting it to my king as only women can, I kept his spirit high and would have done my part on the battlefield had he not made me stay.

Nefertare:

These are indeed strange times, sister. These many years it is that the High Priest makes campaigns in the Palestine to blot out the shameful Hyksos period with more blood. Meanwhile the Kerma clans; strong in their alliance and sensing the weakened position of our land, are pressing at our doors.

Ahmes:

> Indeed. I fear the Kush; did our two peoples not come from the same Ethiope mother lead by Aser and Isis, to settle in Kush and later the land of Kemet to create these two great civilizations on the banks of the Nile, a gift from Re. The same blood flows in our veins, we fight brothers and sisters long removed through time and it is this I fear.

Nefertare:

> Yet should they succeed in this then is Kemet lost. They envy and despise all that we stand for; our position and our wealth, our beliefs. There will be no hope for our peoples should they gain

Ahmes:

> No hope at all; for only a true Pharaoh can rule its peoples. It is this reason why we struggle against all for we protect that which we know and that which defines us. Yet in their desperation I sense a will rather to share in Kemet's glories and to free themselves. Have our peoples not always been linked in war and peace, against the Libyan and other foreign hordes, in building peace, honoring of our gods, and the construction of our mighty

temples and cities. Should they consider themselves subservient to any, are they not equally proud.

Nefertare:

Indeed our subjugation of them has been long but this happens sister between the weak and strong. We do make them stronger by association and yet they will ever rise until they are free.

Ahmes:

This is a people's right, sister.

Nefertare:

But why the discomfort with this Kemet rule I see more advantage than disadvantage

Ahmes:

The answers I am sure may be many, but this I have: that they have no identity in our eyes and therefore seek their own. We treat all as our subjects and expect to be worshiped as true masters but ever are they foreign to the realm. All peoples represent their gods as a likeness of themselves and have needs of kings and queens as a likeness of themselves; this is but nature. I have travelled much and I have seen such with my eyes. The Kush have needs as yet unfulfilled having no outlet to true self-expression. Our art, as seen; must elevate the Kemet above all others; to command respect and fear as does our gods and must convey our greatness and our difference. This I believe is true, as I believe that which has been passed on to us from our forebears; that the Ethiope is the mother of us both.

Nefertare:

I thank you sister as always for your thoughts.

Ahmes:

That we may better understand one another is important, sister. Nania lighten up this mood!

[Nania singing. Enter messenger]

Messenger:

Oh Great High Priestess, King's Mother does request your presence in the throne room

Nefertare:

Tell King's Mother I shall attend shortly.

[Exit messenger]

Nefertare:

> Sister I take my leave sister, we shall speak another time.

> [Exit Nefertare]

Ahmes:

> Come, Mansoo, Chupa, your Queen needs you to fill her tonight as only a Kushite can.

Manservants:

> Such is your bidding Queen's Daughter

> [Nania continues to play soft music as the curtain closes on the love scene]

Act 2 Scene 2

Λ wᴀʀ ʀᴏᴏм wiᴛʜin ᴛʜᴇ pᴀʟᴀᴄᴇ ᴀᴛ Wᴀsᴇᴛ

[Present are Queen Aahotep, Nefertare, Commander Turi, Councillor and guards]

Aahotep:

How stands the situation commander?

Turi:

Sixty lost this day, among them Turi's son. The north side nearly breached but holding. Their bowmen give us much trouble and are fierce. Our stores are much depleted and our soldiers weary.

Aahotep:

Are they for talk, what demands have they?

Councillor:

They seek the recognition of the kingdom of Kush: that land uniting all the peoples of Ta-Sety. They claim too that a false kingship takes seat in Kemet and wish to evoke the King's challenge; a King's worthiness must be judged.

Aahotep:

And what benefits Kemet and the King?

Councillor:

They spoke only of civil peace and continued tributes to the King.

Aahotep:

Without the protection of this land the Libyan, or the Ethiope in the south would have long overrun them. Their existence must they owe to us. Our wealth is used for the worship of our gods and the protection of our land. What good their wealth if transferred overseas or to a peoples unsympathetic of their ways. However, for their good services to us in times of war, we can reduce the tributes they must pay and make more investments in their land. As to the other points we cannot grant, for to give up our hold would let another grasp.

Councillor:

They claim they need protection when the realm is weak and need the recognition of their kingship.

They know that we are divided due to the campaign in Palestine.

Nefertare:

Who speaks for them?

Councillor:

They have one who calls himself Nedjeh and maintains the people's loyalty with a priestly blessing.

Nefertare:

I would like to meet with him face to face that I might know what man he is, what say you King's Mother?

Aahotep:

Daughter the way is yours, my ways are sometimes hard but always fair. Command and rule must be obeyed; we cannot let these rebel leaders think that we are weak. I say we hold.

Nefertare:

I will meet with this king but not from fear. Say I come to spare them more destruction and that if he were a true ruler of men then should he give me audience. Go!

[Exit Councillor]

Aahotep:

    I retire daughter and hope this move goes well.

Nefertare:

    So too I mother for both our peoples.

[Exit all except Nefertare]

Indeed, have we not profited from the Kush. As a civilization older than our own were we not taught and did we not profit from their skill and from their wealth and grew whilst they stood still. Often the great having built are left behind forgot as others push to excel, remembered only in vague whispers the contributions made by them. Time dilutes, separates, fades the memory and pressurises rash activities and sometimes few praise. They may indeed have cause for grievance; for can one speak of them when struck dumb with the glory that is Kemet. The aspirations of commoners will decide our fate and to proceed along the road that makes a peoples great we cannot ignore this fact. The occupations, terrible as they were, have also served to fortify our will; for having been on the precipice of destruction we are concentrated in our will to rebuild and we must use this renewed vigor to lay peace. Yet, should they not think us weak that we make this move? Forwards! A change of pace requires another step

Act 2 Scene 3

In a settlement tent some distance from Waset

[Enter Nedjeh, Councillors to Nedjeh, Priest Tetian, Nefertare and bodyguards]

Nedjeh:

That you have come this day is good, King's Sister.

Nefertare:

That you should receive me in the midst of these hostilities is also good. What chief are you?

Nedjeh:

I am king of the peoples of Kerma from those areas of Ta-Sety unventured by the Kemet. I rule a peoples struggling for identity in a kingdom dispersed.

Nefertare:

But you have no kingdom chief.

Nedjeh:

>A kingdom had we always My Lady; and a line of kings much older than your own. For many years now the Kush has helped the Kemet rise; to fall when she falls but never to rise as far as she. We say this is not right.

Nefertare:

>Who is so brave to stand against the gods' vassal on this earth?

Nedjeh:

>I king Nedjeh for our peoples demand it so.

Priest Tetian:

>The priesthood supports this adventure; spiritual and mental freedom from Kemet are a necessity for our growth. We all in Kush agree on this.

Nefertare:

>Well then it is well represented but ill advised. You begin a war you surely cannot win thinking us weakened by our other campaigns. Then you forget the might of this our realm. Did you not see how we have driven out the Asiatics who now quake when our name is only whispered.

Nedjeh:

We are not Asiatics.

Nefertare:

What have the Kush to say of this? How could they accept an insurrection against their king and gods?

Nedjeh:

The people follow the King as subjects because they believe him to be god's vehicle on this earth. But what they follow is the worship of the gods and they believe that through this vassal they will have a path to a greater glory. However, the priesthood assures us of the gods blessing without the king and claim the weakness of the land is because of a false representative. Because of this we suffer; the people hunger, are driven to slavery with no freedoms; he who comes and demands may take a thousand souls. The Kush build nothing, know nothing but what the Kemet knows. There is a history which cannot be saved. The priesthood speaks; that the Kings laws and the Gods laws can be divided and yet the land prosper. I know not but what I see is the need for change. Can the Kemet change?

Nefertare:

> I see . . . the priests. Know you that the priests lie!

Priest Tetian:

> The lie my lady is in the interpretation of the will of the gods. Was it the will of the gods that the Asiatics should bring Kemet down? For was this uprising not allowed? Did they not settle and were accepted with open arms, until they rose up and fortified their base? Was this god's plan? That the king should be powerless would by conclusion weaken God. Thus this King-God relationship is for the people confusing. How might we correct this so that when the king fails and the land suffers there is still then hope for the people spiritually?

Nefertare:

> The people follow land and religion as one incorporated in one body so is it when they follow into battle. Separate this and conflicts will arise; What is a King? From whence comes kingly power and abilities? Do the Gods command this of me or my King and which should I follow? Know you My Lord has chased off the rebels but only with the blessing of the gods. Had he not this then surely he would have failed, so like our brother did before

him and so like our father. That a king should fail is not the sign of weakness on his part but more the design of the gods bringing humility where once there was boastfulness. For do we not become much stronger after failing and then succeeding appreciating more that which was seemingly lost but then regained. These rogue priests blind the peoples and are not for peace but power; your will is to reduce his Highness to nothing but a symbol and control all his people.

Priest Tetian:

We too are symbols

Nedjeh:

This may be so, but symbols or not the peoples of Kush are now tired of the Kemet hold and seek true independence. They want the benefits of their own labours and true self-government so when Kemet falls they also do not fall.

Nefertare:

And when Kemet rises you also will not rise and left alone cannot beat back the foe. They come each time stronger and stronger still with new techniques and weaponry. If they can conquer us, then what of you? Standing together is the only hope, apart there is none. We have as much need of you as you of us because of the Ethiope to the south and the Libyans to the West and the white sea hoards. My brother, rewards those who serve him and understands their needs and brings fresh hope. We are descended from those, whose quest it was to struggle for the glory of this land and we have learnt our lesson these past years. Join us in this fresh beginning as brothers and sisters that we are. Set not our two great peoples against each other but rather let us advance together.

Nedjeh:

You speak with persuasion but do not address the problems of our land; the lack of leadership. The king makes campaigns in the Palestine and we are left weakened. This centralisation does not help our peoples. We must have the power to shape our future.

Nefertare:

Power alone is not enough, alliances are far stronger. I feel my king may too have a sympathetic ear. My Majesty is of a newer type and may support to a certain extent your claims. I shall put your case before him but only if you cease with these hostilities for we are not ready to let our walls fall and soon our armies will return from far off wars and strengthen our numbers still further. If you reject this we shall crush you and you and we will gain in reality nothing.

Nedjeh:

I am much impressed with your spirit. We are ever ready to discuss peace and are like you adverse to acts of war save in defense or as necessity demands. But we cannot wait until you "chat" with Ahmose. If there is nothing you can offer us to halt these hostilities and satisfy our folk than Kemet will fall for we are a people fighting for our survival and that alone will ensure our victory. Come, let us discuss this further under more favorable conditions.

[Exit all]

Act 3 Scene 1

In a tent on the Sharuhen battlefield in Palestine. The campaign is in its 6ᵗʰ year. Ahmoses army is nearing victory. There are sounds of warfare

[Enter Ahmose, Turi and Scribe]

Ahmose:

I sense the battle will soon be won.

Turi:

Indeed, their spirit like their walls begin to weaken. Their men exhausted by fatigue and lack of food are not so hardy. These many years have seen the enemy beaten back to this his stronghold. Should this fall we never shall be troubled by them again and this end is near.

Ahmose:

Well then the end is near, after so many years. But we shall not leave this ground without much slaughter; so that forever when they recall this time it is with fear. For to dare incursion against our mighty peoples must be hard punished and for the shame of these many years past must they be scarred. Spare but some hundreds for Re's work the rest shall be damned; I will a river of blood to wash away the shameful stain. Let it be so.

Turi:

They shall be sorely punished, the men are true.

Ahmose:

Well that I know it and they shall see great rewards in this adventure. All shall benefit from this glorious victory. Go now and instruct the men to do well this work to please the gods.

[Exit Turi]

And we must quickly put this matter behind us for the reports from Kemet are not favourable and speak of much trouble from the peoples of Ta-Sety. Therefore, our force is needed to defend our lands. Well did they choose this moment to attack but should they think us weak then they are wrong. Also, there is the healing of the land; we must address the people with new hope. I hear my mother and my sister keep the peoples morale with valiant words of encouragement, appealing to their nobility and their pride yet this conflict brings me much uneasiness.

[Enter Servant]

Servant:

A messenger is come from Kemet

Ahmose:

He shall enter.

Messenger:

I bring news from Kings Sister, High Priestess Ahmose-Nefertare

Ahmose:

[Reading]:

Brother, we fear and all is not calm. Though I have spoken with the Kushite rebels they will not cease hostilities until we guarantee the Kush self rule. Be quick in your return that we might discuss a truce.

Great Kings Sister High Priestess Ahmose-Nefertare

71

What! Never shall I concede the land of Kush! Shall I be the first of Kemet's kings to lose this land? I must quickly back to Kemet before this idea becomes too popular. Serf fetch me Commander Turi.

[Exit servant]

We will away back to Kemet to exact a mighty blow to these Kushite rebels.

[Enter Turi]

Turi:

My King?

Ahmose:

We must quickly return to defend our land. The Asiatics shall be spared to fight our fight should they not yield so should they die.

Turi:

Then none shall die if they serve our cause.

Ahmose:

Good, we divide the men I go ahead and you come after. One third shall rest with you. Instruct them of our quest; that we make march to Kush to quell the rebel spirit in that land.

Turi:

Yes, My Majesty. I also have a reckoning with these chiefs

Ahmose:

Yes, your son. I did forget, my sorrows go to you.

Turi:

No matter, he died a soldier's death. I shall communicate the command.

[Exit Turi]

Here scribe.

Scribe:

My Majesty

Ahmose:

Let the record show of the great victory at Sharuhen with many taken and much slaughter. Write of the bravery of our soldiers and that each man shall receive a reward commensurate with his standing in the army. Let it be noted of the threat to Kemet and that we march to Kush to squash the rebel uprising in that land. That is all.

Scribe:

It shall be marked, My Majesty.

[Exit Scribe]

Ahmose:

Go Scribe. Now is a time for feats not words though mighty is your craft. Mark victories and bloody deeds, mark bold commands and reckless acts. All matters. When action is still, as bodies mummified, so lives your art. Foreign eyes will seek to understand our ways, perceive our lives as though of yesterday and they will wonder at this peoples through your words. Therefore, go scribe.

[Exit]

Act 3 Scene 2

Battlefield near the Fortress of Waset

[Present are Nedjeh, his sons and guards. Ahmose, Nefertere and their guards arrive in chariots]

Ahmose:

Chief, I am here and you should now fear. Subject yourself and spare the lives of your men. We have no quarrel with a peoples who have served us well but you must subject yourself to our rule.

Nedjeh:

Young King, I had hoped to be inside those walls before our meet. What you see spread from that hill to that is the sum anger of your rule these many hundred years. The depths of that anger you cannot see. Should I go back to those seeking change, freedom from servitude and suffering and say the King speaks and you must leave. Must we quake, must we follow.

Ahmose:

> No, you should return and say: Ahmose mighty ruler of the proud Kemet, recent subjecter of the Asiatics, cleanser of these lands requests your continued subjugation or your deaths. Do you not see the armies spread before you, swelled with those we have conquered.

Nedjeh:

> I see two armies but not one soul; you subject a peoples and hope that in the fray of battle they will die for you with no gain. This army cannot win.

Nefertare:

> King, though we spoke much and understood our reasons we find ourselves at this point. One will lose and the other will gain much. Am I not an honorary princess and can this honour persuade you to change your course.

Nedjeh:

> I am not so weak to feel I can be bent by the simple words of a princess, however honoured. What you see before you in my person and my sons is a strength and will formidable and unbending. The right we see on our side will shake the Kemet, remould

your thinking and readjust your actions. After this campaign, you shall no longer be yourselves; for either you shall rule two kingdoms or shall we. Measure these words well young King.

Ahmose:

Then have we gained a kingdom

Nedjeh:

So have you lost one

[Exit all]

Act 3 Scene 3

A room at Waset

[Enter King Ahmose, Nefertare, Queen Aahotep, Servant]

Ahmose:

>We return King's Mother to let you know of the great slaughter enacted on the Kush; our soldiers have put the rebels down hard and pushed them back as far as Buhen. There they hold firm. But onslaught after onslaught will see their end.

Nefertare:

>I would it had another end. Know you that we should seek to win the loyalty of these people and this not through war.

Aahotep:

>Loyalty daughter! Fear and respect is all a king demands from his subjects. They must bend before us in honour and recognition of our might.

Nefertare:

That they do already.

Ahmose:

Nay, sister for had they this they never would have sought this course.

Nefertare:

Desperation does drive us to defy many things. Fear and respect alone are not enough to secure a lasting peace, unless this is not the objective that you seek. If in some short time you will another uprising, fueled by burning resentment and stronger than the last, then this indeed is the policy you must hold. If, however, you will that people speak your name as one who brought real and substantial peace then must you bend.

Ahmose:

Did Kamose bend, my father Tao, his father and his too? Ever could we hold the rebels still.

Nefertare:

And ever have we had rebellions! Now is the time for discussion not war. What they demand is nothing which they cannot take perhaps not today or tomorrow but sometime in the future. What you do by the ignorance of their will is pass the problem on to another. Meet this difficulty head to head and people will remark this wonderment; for making peace is harder still than making war.

Ahmose:

And you sister had in mind a deal, what benefits Kemet?

Nefertare:

A free exchange is better than the taking at knife point. In brief their officials receive more authorities but we remain the sovereigns of both lands with continued tributes to the king. This was my idea brother to lay a foundation for the future.

Aahotep:

I see it not. More power, later to be used against us.

Nefertare:

Not if we speak of peace and make our pacts. We have much to do in Kemet alone.

Ahmose:

Yes sister, I do recall the words of the All-Knowing One:

> *Seek not temptation of another's house,*
> *Rejoice in this earth from which life comes,*

Nefertare:

These are indeed wise words

Ahmose:

But the land of Kush sister is not *another's* home.

Nefertare:

We must recognise the sovereignty of their land. Think back to Hut-waret and the address to Apopi; in which we spoke of a people's rights and dignities. Is this not so for the peoples of Ta-Sety?

Ahmose:

But in this deal the priests will win, dividing king and god and king and people!

Nefertare:

Then hold the priests in check but not the populace.

Ahmose:

That I shall do sister, that I shall do. How is your relation with this Kerma king?

Nefertare:

> This is good. I felt I had gained trust and respect. I found him just. He honored me, he said, as he would a Kushite princess in recognition of my quest for peace. But he did warn me of the folly of my ways knowing too well the hearts of men.

Ahmose.

> A Kushite princess but Queen of Kemet and much more. Serf, I will send a message. This message to Commander Turi to pull our soldiers back to Kemet's borders and instruct the men to the collection of rewards for this and other battles fought. That is all.

[Exit servant]

The business of our marriage shall come first and than the affairs of state

[Exit all]

Act 3 Scene 4

A sun temple in Waset

[Enter Priest Ani and priestesses]

Priest Ani:

Our fortunes ride the ill winds, my sisters; my cousin Tetian was slain and the Kush driven back. We must flee to save our lives.

First Priestess:

Is there no hope, my lord?

Second Priestess:

We tried and did not this time succeed. But there ever will be hope whilst we remain strong.

First Priestess:

How might we escape?

Priest Ani:

>This night those loyal to us will aid us in our flight with passage to that part of Kush still safe from Ahmose' hand.

First Priestess:

>But have we not failed?

Priest Ani:

>This struggle is but one of many that will see the king and gods divide. It is but only a question of time.

>[Enter Commander Turi and two soldiers]

Turi:

>Here are the traitors seeking sanctuary, or do you make your prayers priests? Know you that we have learned of your treachery; the traitor Tetian to save his life spoke of your involvement in these events. His admission did not save him but has damned you. Your punishments will be swift. Take the witches and dispatch them but make sure they are stained before they meet their journey's end.

Priestesses:

>No! Father save us!

[Soldiers drag priestesses off, screams can be heard offstage]

Priest Ani:

Are you men or beasts, do not torture these maidens!

Turi:

Silence priest they are done for and like you have deserved their fate. Perhaps you a have some words to explain your folly?

[Offstage: screams]

Priest Ani:

Our actions need not your understanding. Soldiers obey and do not question their masters. How can a willing slave hope to understand the subtleties of our struggle for freedom.

Turi:

We are all commanded men. You chose to have two masters, we have but one. Your understanding of a soldier's intelligence points to your defeat. The might lies in these arms and had you swayed those you may not now be staring at oblivion. You sought another master and have paid a price

[Offstage: screams, soldiers laughing]

Priest Ani:

>Our time on this earth is finite but time in the realm of Re is eternal. Here sits no true Pharaoh no godhood was earned here. The Gods do not err and the reign of Ahmose will not keep Kemet safe

Turi:

>Should we fall then should we fall together a peoples must rise and fall as one. Your poison divides and by this division destroys all hopes of unity, setting brother against brother. This is not what the Gods chose for Kemet, this is not the teachings of Re. Have you not seen Our Majesty's successes. Surely this points to godliness. How could you priest have been so full of hopelessness and doubt

Priest Ani:

>My son you still do not see. Ours is an awakening not an act of desperation. Too long have we slept hoping and praying for the god in man to guide us. That Ahmose should rise without a godly blessing angered the gods. The Gods are never changing ever constant, man is weak.

Turi:

> No! Power fueled your treacherous activities.
> Ever were you envious of the omnipotence of His
> Majesty, frustrated with your perceived weakness
> you sought to steal his power. This also gave Tetian
> to our understanding.

> [Re-enter soldiers]

First Soldier:

> They are dispatched.

Turi:

> And so too Ani

> [Turi kills Priest]

> We shall make examples of these traitors for any
> who should try to break that greatest ever bond
> that exists between a Pharaoh and his Gods

> [Exit all]

Act 3 Scene 5

Throne room at Waset. It has been 10 years since the Hyksos were expelled

[Ahmose and Nefertare seated on their thrones]

Ahmose:

> Peace reigns in the land of Kemet as predicted queen. Our further campaigns have secured a peace and security from those seeking our demise. In Ta-Sety there reigns peace too as the Kush are appeased with greater authorities. The links between our peoples is good as you did wish. Nedjeh is lost to warfare but his son rules and has agreed to continue royalties for more freedoms. I know your thoughts; that I acted rashly but when I survey the calm, can this be right? Had I been able to achieve the same with peace? Look now, we reign as king and queen over two kingdoms: this Kingdom of Kemet and this Kingdom of Kush in peace.

Nefertare:

>Indeed, and I see there is a healing and a foundation for lasting peace.

Ahmose:

>The priesthood who aided us is rewarded and those who were set against us are humbled with the death of the traitors who did seek to steal my godliness for their own. How blind and foolish to think the peoples could accept such a parting.

Nefertare:

>Had this occurred then were you no longer sovereign. For only the son of Re can reign supreme.

Ahmose:

>We reign supreme now and shall for a thousand years and after years, for I sister have married you, my Kushite princess. Now I do recall a King Mother's dream.

Nefertare:

>A mother's dream, My Majesty?

Ahmose:

> Of late I have been wondering at our line; this perfect blood that has again engendered peace reuniting a torn land.

Nefertare:

> What means, My Majesty? What has come into your heart?

Ahmose:

> I have recalled the mother of my mother and the mother of my father, Kings Great Wife and King's Mother, Tetisheri now dead. A tomb-chamber and a sepulcher of hers are at this moment lain upon the Abju soil. I recall her name because I wish to honour her with a pyramid and a chapel in the Sacred Land close to the monument of My Majesty. This is how My Majesty wishes to recognise the contributions of this queen. This is how My Majesty wishes to acknowledge the contributions of this sex.

[Exit]